Chopper Cycle Mania

By Ed and Ruth Radlauer

AN ELK GROVE BOOK

CHILDRENS PRESS, CHICAGO

STRATEGIES, a teaching guide for using *MANIA BOOKS* for reading instruction, is available along with a cassette recording and *MANIA CARDS* (skill-builders) to accompany this book.

Photo credits:
    Robin Radlauer, page 24

Library of Congress Cataloging in Publication Data

Radlauer, Edward.
    Chopper cycle mania.
    (Mania books)
    "An Elk Grove book."
    SUMMARY: An easy-to-read introduction to two-
and three-wheel motorcycles.
    1. Motorcycles—Juvenile literature.
[1. Motorcycles] I. Radlauer, Ruth Shaw, joint
author. II. Title.
TL440.R26   629.2'275   80-12261
ISBN 0-516-07779-1

A RADLAUER

Mania Book

CREATED FOR CHILDRENS PRESS BY
*RADLAUER PRODUCTIONS INCORPORATED

Chopper cycle mania?

Yes, it's chopper
cycle mania.

Your chopper needs wheels.

It needs big wheels.

Your chopper needs—

—two big wheels.

Yes, your chopper needs
two big wheels.

Two big wheels?

A three-wheel chopper—

—needs three big wheels.

Your three-wheel chopper
needs one wheel in front—

—and two big wheels
in the back.

Yes, a three-wheel chopper—

—needs two wheels in the back?

Your chopper cycle
needs a seat.

A chopper may have
one big seat.

Your chopper may have
one big seat.

And your chopper may have
a seat for a friend.

Yes, all choppers
have seats.

All choppers have seats?

A chopper needs
an engine.

A chopper needs
a big engine.

Your chopper needs a big
engine and a gas tank.

All choppers have
big engines and gas tanks.

All chopper cycles have
big engines?

All chopper cycles have
big gas tanks?

Chopper cycle mania?

Yes, it's chopper
cycle mania.

Chopper Words